Real HEROES WEAR JEANS

5-Minute Devotions for Kids

by Tim Hansel

Chariot Books™
David C. Cook Publishing Co.

Published by Chariot Books™,
an imprint of David C. Cook Publishing Co.
David C. Cook Publishing Co., Elgin, Illinois 60120
David C. Cook Publishing Co., Weston, Ontario

REAL HEROES WEAR JEANS
© 1989 by Tim Hansel

Unless otherwise noted, all Scripture quotations in this publication are from
the Holy Bible, New International Version. Copyright © 1973, 1978, 1984,
International Bible Society.

Verses marked (TLB) are taken from *The Living Bible* © 1971, owned by
assignment by Illinois Regional Bank N.A. (as trustee). Used by permission of
Tyndale House Publishers Inc., Wheaton, IL 60189. All rights reserved.

Cover and interior design by Elizabeth Thompson.
Illustrations by Joe Van Severen.

First Printing, 1989
Printed in the United States of America
93 92 91 90   5 4 3 2

Library of Congress Cataloging-in-Publication Data

Hansel, Tim.
    Real heroes wear jeans.

    Summary: Presents prayers, Bible verses, and brief stories of individuals
whose religious beliefs gave them the courage to overcome hardships and
handicaps.
    1. Children—Prayer-books and devotions—English. [1. Prayer books and
devotions] I. Van Severen, Joe, ill. II. Title.
BV4870.H26   1989   242'.62   89-9953
ISBN 1-55513-333-9

TABLE OF
CONTENTS

STOP!
Read this first . . .

Have you ever wanted to be a hero. . .or at least brave enough to do what none of your friends dared to do? If you were a hero, people might use words like brave, gutsy, daring, courageous, and fearless, to describe you.

Some kids think heroes are only in comic books or maybe playing football for the 49ers, or making lots of money in a rock band. But real heroes are people like the friends you'll meet in this book. And when you've thought about it, I think you'll see how you can be a hero, too. That's why I've written this book. The world needs young people who know how to live like heroes. I hope you will be one of those young people who is willing to go on a real hero adventure.

Tim Hansel

HERO PRACTICE:

Some kids might say, "I don't know how I could ever be a hero." The section marked "Hero Practice" will help you find out what it feels like for you to be a *real* hero.

TAKE COURAGE:

God's Word is full of words of courage. When you see "Take Courage," a Bible verse will give you courage to be the hero God wants you to be.

PRAYER:

Sometimes it's difficult to pray. You want to say something to God, but don't know where to start. The prayers in this book will help you get started. Then you can add whatever you want to say to God.

ANSWER CHECK:

Make a check in the box when your prayer is answered. One of the best ways to build up your courage is to look back through the book and see how many prayers God has already answered.

Your words are important!

We've left you extra room throughout this book so you can write or draw your thoughts and ideas. Have fun!

About Tim Hansel . . .

Tim Hansel has done things most of us only dream about. He's sailed 25,000 miles on the Pacific Ocean in a forty-three-foot boat. He's climbed one of the highest mountains in the United States. He's worked with some of the toughest gangs in New York City, helping gang members get to know Jesus Christ.

After coaching high school soccer and college football, Tim started Summit Expedition, an organization that takes kids and adults on wilderness and mountain-climbing trips. One of the most exciting Summit programs is GO FOR IT, especially for handicapped people.

That's Not Fair!

If you stop and listen to kids on the playground or in your backyard, you might hear the words, "That's not fair!"

Bob Wieland had as much right as anyone to use those words when he stepped on a land mine and his legs were blown off in Viet Nam. He had been a good athlete and could have gone back to a promising career in professional baseball. When the medics picked him up from the battle area, he was so badly hurt that they tagged him DOA (dead on arrival). But they didn't count on Bob's courage and faith in God. He surprised everyone by living and leaving the hospital in record time. Never once did he way, "That's not fair! I was a good athlete. I needed my legs." Rather, he said, "God knows what He is doing, and He had a better plan for my life."

Bob was right. Through his efforts he has raised more than $300,000 for needy people and gotten a lot of people thinking about God. Wherever he goes, he encourages people. He says, "Through faith in God, determination, and dedication, there is nothing within the will of God a person can't achieve."

6

HERO PRACTICE:

Right now you can probably think of at least two things that aren't fair. How can you turn those unfair things around like Bob Wieland did? How could God change those unfair things into something good?

TAKE COURAGE:

"And we know that in all things God works for the good of those who love him, who have been called according to his purpose." Romans 8:28

PRAYER:

It makes me feel a lot better, God, to know that You are here with me. Please help me to see how You can change the unfair things into something good.

ANSWER CHECK:

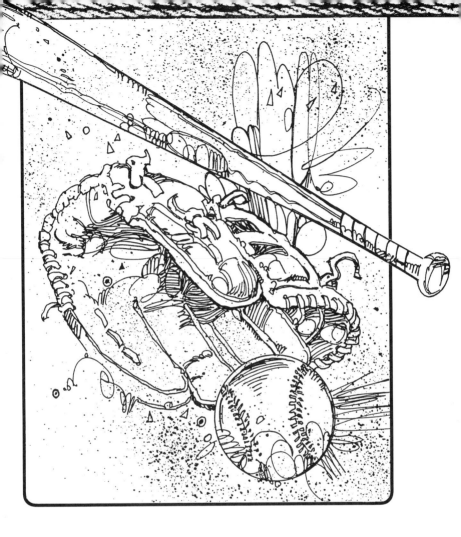

Real heroes. . .
trust God to take care of them when things aren't fair.

A Day to Say, "Thank You"

Because of only two minutes without oxygen when she was born, Pam Dahl will spend her life in a wheelchair. She will never walk, and she is unable to do many of the everyday tasks we take for granted.

That's why it's so amazing to learn that Pam has graduated from college and is now working on her master's degree.

Most surprising of all is that Pam *never* complains. She has what I would call a "grateful heart." She is so thankful that God loves her. That's how she keeps that beautiful smile on her face. And that's why she is one of my heroes.

HERO PRACTICE:

You can probably think of many things to complain about every day–parents always reminding you of chores, brothers and sisters who won't leave you alone. Maybe it's your hair, too curly or sticks up where it shouldn't. Just for one day try saying "thank you" instead of complaining, and see how you feel by the end of the day.

TAKE COURAGE:

"Give thanks in all circumstances, for this is God's will for you in Christ Jesus."

I Thessalonians   5:18

PRAYER:

Lord, I have a lot to be thankful for. Here are some of the things I'm thinking about right now:

ANSWER CHECK:

Real heroes. . .
remember to tell God "Thank You."

The Strongest Man in the World

When I was in grade school I thought being a Christian was just for "sissies." If you were a Christian, you were probably a weak person.

In college, I went to a meeting with a bunch of other football and rugby players like myself and met Paul Anderson. He weighed 300 pounds and was all muscle. During the meeting, he had about twenty of us guys come up front and get on a table. Then he got under it and lifted us all up! He then stood up, looked at the group and said quietly, "I'm the strongest man in the world." (He really is. He holds the world's record for lifting the most weight, which is 6,270 pounds!) "But," he said, "I couldn't make it through a day without the power of Jesus Christ. If I'm not embarrassed to say that, I don't know why any of you should be."

Paul is one of my heroes because he wasn't ashamed to be a Christian, and because he helped me decide to give my life to Jesus Christ.

HERO PRACTICE:

It takes courage to be a Christian and stand up for what you know is right. If you've been ashamed to be known as a Christian as I was, ask God for courage today.

TAKE COURAGE:

"I am not ashamed of the gospel, because it is the power of God for the salvation of everyone who believes." Romans 1:16

PRAYER:

Thank You for courage, Lord. I need courage to be a Christian. Help me not to be ashamed to stand up for what is right.

ANSWER CHECK:

Real heroes...
are not ashamed of being known as a Christian.

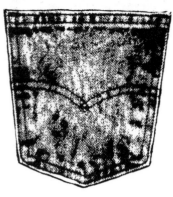

Go for It!

We could see for miles as we slowly climbed up one of the toughest rock climbs in the Sierras—"The Prow." It was 800 feet of sheer rock to the top. And when you rappelled[1] off the top to a small ledge 150 feet below, you felt as though you had jumped off a ten-story building. It's a scary experience for anyone, and today Sherry was trying it for the first time. The incredible thing was that Sherry couldn't walk. Her disease, called muscular dystrophy,[2] kept her from doing many things. But she was determined to learn to climb mountains. With the help of some of the guys on the Summit staff, she had gotten this far, and now she was doing what no other disabled person had ever done—she was rappelling off "The Prow," laughing all the way down.

This was no surprise to any of us. Sherry had found in God the courage to love herself as she is and live life as fully as possible. That's why when she heard about our GO FOR IT mountain climbing program for the disabled, she said, "I'm gonna go."

HERO PRACTICE:

All of us have certain characteristics that we see as "handicaps"—a nose that's too big, clumsy feet, shy personality, etc. What is your handicap? Remember, God can help you love yourself just the way you are.

TAKE COURAGE:

"I praise you because I am fearfully and wonderfully made; your works are wonderful, I know that full well." Psalm 139:14

[1] Rappel: to lower yourself down a cliff by ropes that are attached to your harness and to the top of the cliff.
[2] Muscular dystrophy: a hereditary disease characterized by gradual weakening of muscles.

 **PRAYER:**

Dear God, there are certain things about myself that I wish were different. Help me to learn to love even that part of me the way You do.

ANSWER CHECK:

Real heroes...

are learning to like themselves as they are.

A Real Friend

I don't know about you, but sometimes when I'm with someone who can do things a lot better than I can, I feel yucky about myself. That's why my friend Jack Meyer is a real hero to me.

Jack is just the right weight and he's strong. These days I'm kind of overweight and not so strong. Jack is a good athlete. Before I had a mountain-climbing accident it was easy for me to be a good athlete, too. Now it's very hard.

But when Jack and I go to a gym to work out together, he won't let me feel bad about myself. He just encourages me the whole time we're there. He makes me believe that I can do anything if I try. He's a real friend.

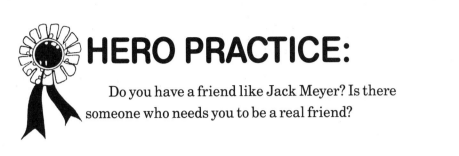

HERO PRACTICE:

Do you have a friend like Jack Meyer? Is there someone who needs you to be a real friend?

TAKE COURAGE:

"A man of many companions may come to ruin, but there is a friend who sticks closer than a brother." Proverbs 18:24

PRAYER:

Dear Lord, thank You for real friends. Help me to be a friend to _____ this week.

ANSWER CHECK:

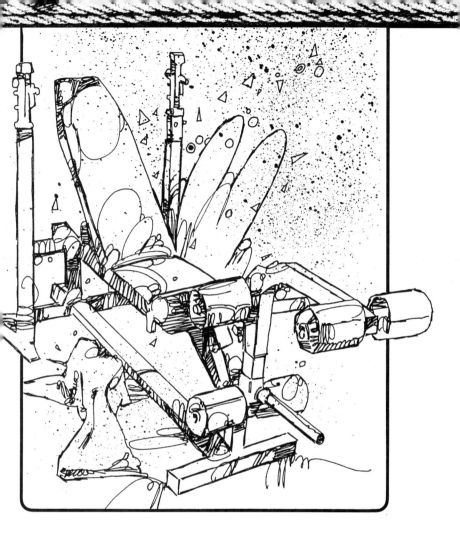

Real heroes...
see the best in others.

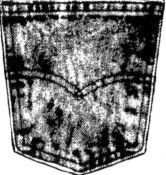

Let's Do It Again!

We pushed Pam Dahl down the trail in her wheelchair to the place where the climb began. Then Amy and Kay lifted her out and helped her to the ground. Jill got behind to push, and Pam started her slow and painful climb up the rough rocks. Pam's disease, called cerebral palsy,[1] kept her from walking or using her hands, but she was determined to get up that mountain. So, with her arms bent back and her feet working like motors trying to find a foothold, she wiggled her body up the mountain. She worked so hard that her face was right against the rock. I turned to look back and heard her saying, "Way to go!" over and over again.

Pam wouldn't give up. It took over two hours for her to reach the top, with Amy, Kay, and Jill helping all the way. So I couldn't believe what she said as she lifted her scratched face and grinned at us. "Let's do it again!"

HERO PRACTICE:

When I remember how Pam wouldn't give up, it makes me try harder to keep going when I want to quit. Think of something you have to do that makes you feel like quitting.

TAKE COURAGE:

"Be strong and courageous. . . Do not be afraid or discouraged, for the Lord God, my God, is with you."

I Chronicles 28:20

---

[1] Cerebral palsy: a disability that affects muscle coordination.

 **PRAYER:**

It's hard to keep going when I feel like quitting, Lord. Thank You for being there to help.

ANSWER CHECK:

Real heroes...
never stop trying.

A Teacher You Can Count On

Kids at Whittier Christian High School in California are getting used to seeing a little man in a large, shiny wheelchair zip through the halls on his way to class. Zane Mills is the math and science teacher—the one with the great sense of humor and the one that kids know they can count on. He listens to them. They know that Zane really cares, and he'll do anything he can to encourage them.

Zane is a hero. His disability makes it so hard for him to do even the simplest things that nobody would blame him if he just used his energy on himself all day. But Zane loves the Lord, and he has decided that living for God means really loving people. That's what he does.

HERO PRACTICE:

It's easy to forget that being a Christian means loving other people. What loving things could you do for your family this week?. . . For your friends?

TAKE COURAGE:

"A new command I give you: Love one another. As I have loved you, so you must love one another."

John 13:34

 **PRAYER:**

I know at least one person, Lord, who needs to be loved. Help me think of what I can do to love that person.

ANSWER CHECK:

Real heroes...
show their love
for others.

Old Chevy or New Corvette?

If you had your choice between a new Corvette and a beat-up old Chevy, you'd probably be like most people. You'd choose the Corvette. Or, what if you could choose to make either $100,000 or $15,000 a year? What would you choose? Well, that's not hard. You would choose $100,000, of course. Then why would someone choose the old beat-up car and less money if they didn't have to? That's what makes Craig Schindler a hero.

I met Craig in college. He was one of the most brilliant students there, and one of the most popular. He was always staying up half the night listening to someone's problems. Craig went on to become a university professor, a lawyer, and a psychologist. But Craig was very concerned about what might happen to kids like you if someone didn't start talking about big issues like preventing nuclear war and saving our environment. So he organized a group called "Project Victory" that gets important people together to talk seriously about the future. He doesn't make much money and he drives a beat-up old car, but Craig is happiest doing what he knows is the most important job for him.

HERO PRACTICE:

Right now, you probably don't think much about the future—when you will be grown up. God wants to prepare you to make good choices as a grown-up. Ask Him to help you get ready now for the future He has planned for you.

TAKE COURAGE:

"Trust in the Lord with all your heart and lean not on your own understanding; in all your ways acknowledge him, and he will make your paths straight." Proverbs 3:5, 6

 **PRAYER:**

The future seems a long way off, Lord, but help me get ready for it now. Help me to make good choices.

ANSWER CHECK:

Real heroes . . .
know what's really important in life.

I'll Go Anywhere, Except...

Mike Edwards is a modern-day Jonah. He grew up as a farm kid who didn't know anything about the city. In college, when he got serious about being a Christian, he said, "God, You can do anything with my life, except I don't want to go into the inner city, and I don't want to work with poor people."

What Mike couldn't see is that God knows each of us far better than we know ourselves. He knew that Mike would actually love working in the inner city with poor people, if he ever had an opportunity to try it. So God arranged a way for Mike to try it.

Today, Mike works in a rescue mission on skid row in Los Angeles, giving food and clothing to the homeless, and teaching them the Bible. And there's no place else he'd rather be.

HERO PRACTICE:

Like Mike, you and I sometimes pray, "God, I'll do anything . . . except." How can this prayer change when we remember that God loves us and knows exactly what will make us happy?

TAKE COURAGE:

"The steps of good men are directed by the Lord. He delights in each step they take."

Psalms 37:23, TLB

 # PRAYER:

Dear God, thank You for knowing better than I do exactly what will make me happy. Help me to trust You.

ANSWER CHECK:

Real heroes . . .
trust God with their future.

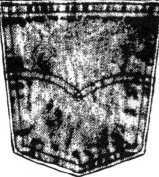

Pedaling in Hawaii

Imagine yourself pedaling your bike down the road in Hawaii. Sound great? Now imagine yourself pedaling 112 miles through blackened lava fields under a scorching sun with vicious winds doing their best to blow you the other way. And imagine that before the bike ride, you had just finished a two-mile swim in the ocean, and when you get off your bike, you'll still have to run twenty-six miles!

That's what you'd have to do if you entered the famous Iron Man Triathlon in Hawaii. And that's what Dr. Ken Campbell did a few years after his body was badly burned in a car crash.

Why did he do something that hard? Because Ken has learned that he feels the best about himself when he decides to do something hard (when he sets a goal) and then does it (finishes the goal). He feels better about the burn scars on his body when he asks his body to do difficult things, and then works hard until his body does them. It all fits in with his greatest goal of all—to live for Jesus Christ every day of his life.

HERO PRACTICE:

What difficult thing could you choose to work on until it's finished? Maybe it's finishing your homework every day this week, or going out for the soccer team and not quitting in the middle of the season. Or maybe you'd like to try racing (start with one or two kilometer races) like Dr. Ken does.

TAKE COURAGE:

"I have fought the good fight, I have finished the race, I have kept the faith." II Timothy 4:7

PRAYER:

Dear God, I don't want to be a quitter. Help me to set goals and keep working on them even when I don't feel like it.

ANSWER CHECK:

Real heroes. . .
set clear goals and go after them.

Joni

Joni was a pretty, happy, active teenager who loved the Lord when she broke her neck in a diving accident. After she was pulled out of the water, she realized that she couldn't feel anything from her neck down. Since that time, Joni's legs and arms have been paralyzed. But instead of feeling sorry for herself, Joni got busy. She learned how to operate a motorized wheelchair. She learned how to feed herself, using her neck muscles and special arm straps. She learned how to drive a specially equipped van. And she even learned how to paint beautiful pictures, holding the brush with her teeth.

I met Joni about four years ago when we talked together about our GO FOR IT program for the physically disabled. I was amazed to hear about the many ways she was helping other disabled people. Joni has learned that a real hero takes the worst that can happen and lets the Lord turn it into something good.

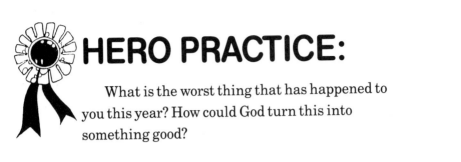

HERO PRACTICE:

What is the worst thing that has happened to you this year? How could God turn this into something good?

TAKE COURAGE:

"Now to him who is able to do immeasurably more than all we ask or imagine, according to his power that is at work within us..." Ephesians 3:20

 # PRAYER:

My worst thing isn't as bad as Joni's, Lord. But sometimes it feels as bad. Thank You that You can turn my worst thing into something good, just as You did for Joni.

ANSWER CHECK:

Real heroes . . .
trust God no matter what happens.

Zac, The Body Builder

My son Zac has always had a fantastic mind for building things. I remember when we bought a new barbecue grill that came all in pieces in a big box—one of those do-it-yourself jobs. It would have taken me a week to figure it out. Zac had it put together in two hours.

One thing Zac hadn't been real successful building was his body. He was a big guy, but a little of his weight wasn't muscle. However, Zac had some important hero qualities—he knew he could do something if he really tried. So, in ninth grade he went to work on his body.

He set a realistic weight-loss goal—twenty pounds, and worked out a plan for exercise. Every day after school he lifted weights and played racquetball at a local gym. In less than six weeks, Zac had reached his goal, and is now setting new goals. It was hard, especially when his brother, who never gains weight, was eating all the "good" stuff Zac loves. But he stayed with the program and now he feels better about himself than ever before.

HERO PRACTICE:

Most of us have trouble sticking with something, especially when it takes a long time. For you it might be piano lessons, or a science project, or even losing weight, like Zac. Remember that God is interested in everything you do, and will help you stick with it.

TAKE COURAGE:

"The Christ you have to deal with is not a weak person outside you, but a tremendous power inside you." II Corinthians 13:3, Phillips

 # PRAYER:

I'm thankful, God, that You care about me so much that You will help me with:

ANSWER CHECK:

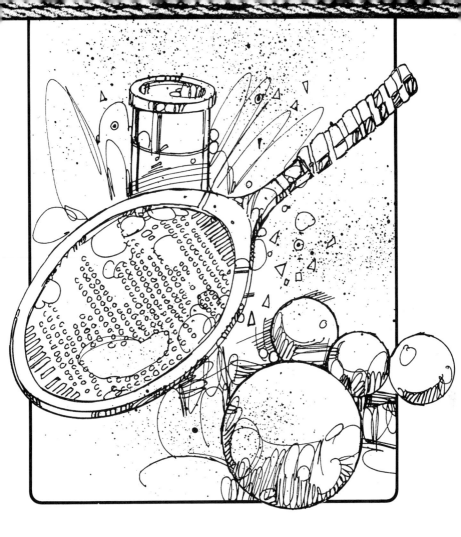

Real heroes . . .
count on God to help them reach their goals.

Oh, Silly Me!

Maybe you're like me. Sometimes I don't even try to do certain things because I'm afraid I'll make a mistake. Then I think of Mark—one of my heroes.

Mark was born without hands. I suppose he could have decided to stay in the house all his life so no one could make fun of him when he made mistakes. Instead, Mark learned to do many things—write, throw a football, play a trombone, play tennis—with the stubs on the ends of his arms. He even went to college where he was an All-American football player, and then became a high school coach.

Sometimes Mark makes mistakes, but he always tries to do his best. And if he messes up, he gets a funny grin on his face and says, "Oh, silly me." Then he tries again.

HERO PRACTICE:

Everybody makes mistakes. It's the people who refuse to let mistakes keep them from trying again who are the real heroes.

TAKE COURAGE:

"In God I trust; I will not be afraid."

Psalm 56:4b

 **PRAYER:**

Dear God, I know You will help me be the best I can be. One thing I need courage for is _____
_____.

Thank You that I don't have to be afraid of making mistakes.

ANSWER CHECK:

Real heroes. . .
don't get discouraged by their mistakes.

Hey, Champ, You Can Do It!

Have you ever heard a kid say, "Hey, stupid. I'll bet your mother dropped you on your head." Sometimes kids (and adults, too) put people down who aren't good at things like sports or math, or they make fun of people who don't dress right.

One of my heroes is Coach Parks. He knows that God made every kid special, and that's how Coach treats everybody. When we were coaching high school sports together, a kid named Henry came out who was not very athletic. He was fifteen, but he looked about ten. And he was usually about forty yards behind everyone else. Coach Parks started running alongside Henry in practice, hollering encouraging words like, "Way to go, Champ!" and "Hey, Champ, you can do it!" Soon Henry began to feel like a real winner, and he ran better than he ever thought he could.

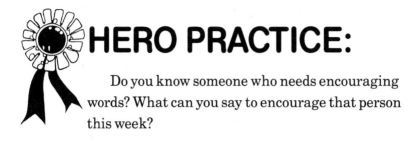

HERO PRACTICE:

Do you know someone who needs encouraging words? What can you say to encourage that person this week?

TAKE COURAGE:

"Therefore encourage one another and build each other up." I Thessalonians 5:11

PRAYER:

Dear God, please help me say encouraging
words to _____ this week.

ANSWER CHECK:

Real heroes. . .
encourage other people.

Do you know any *real heroes*? In what ways have you been a real hero since reading this book? When is it most difficult for you to be a real hero?

Tim Hansel would like to hear your answers to these questions. You can write to him at:

Tim Hansel
c/o Chariot Books
850 N. Grove Ave.
Elgin, IL 60120